Dedication

To my delightful mother
Ethel Yarick Morgan

Acknowledgements

Cicero and I are grateful to Mr. William Stevenson and Mr. Wullie Wilson of St. Cuthbert's Co-operative Association, Edinburgh; to Colonel F. Harry Orr, Commandant, The Royal Army Veterinary Corps Training Centre, Melton Mowbray, and to the following officers and men of Cicero's regiment, The Life Guards: his squadron leader, Major John Fuller, Captain Charles Harcourt-Smith, Captain Christopher D'Oyly, Riding Master Captain Alec Jackson, Squadron Corporal Major Peter Hewett and, in particular, Corporal Barry McKie, Cicero's trainer, and Trooper John Barrass, Cicero's groom, both of whose skill, patience and good humour were vital to Cicero's progress.

We also thank Mr. Clayton Kirkpatrick, Editor of *The Chicago Tribune*, for permission to include in this book a portion of Cicero's story I wrote for *The Tribune*, and the Trustees of the British Museum for permission to reproduce a section of an engraving by Wenceslaus Hollar (1607–1677) showing one of Cicero's early predecessors in King Charles II's procession from the Tower to his London coronation at Westminster Abbey in 1661.

Gwen Morgan

CICERO

and The Silver Drums

AS TOLD TO GWEN MORGAN

with photographs by the author

Arlington Books London

CICERO AND THE SILVER DRUMS
first published 1972 by
Arlington Books (Publishers) Ltd.,
38 Bury Street St James's
London S.W.1

© *Gwen Morgan 1971*

Made and Printed in England
by The Garden City Press Limited
London and Letchworth

ISBN 0 85140 205 4

CICERO
and The Silver Drums

Contents

"Crumbs, I am like a fairy tale character come alive"

1 *The Miracle*

"I know what you are thinking," Cicero the Drum Horse said suddenly.

His voice was deep and kind, just as I would have expected it to be, had I not been so surprised.

"Don't you know that, sometimes, if you wish for something hard enough and then do something about it, your wish comes true?" he went on, his voice having just a touch of the Scottish burr, which years of living in London will probably never soften because he obviously likes it, and savours his words.

Amid all the grandeur of his surroundings, the spacious park with its bridle path, the newest, finest stables in all the world, the touch of Scotland in his speech was all that Cicero had to remind himself of his former home. Even his name was new. I wanted to ask what they had called him in Edinburgh. But I had lost my tongue.

"I don't know why you should be so astonished to hear me speak," Cicero went on, obviously enjoying himself.

"You have gone quite pale! Do have a sugar lump, yourself. You look as if you need one. Don't you remember how in the old days horses flew and saved their masters in battle and did things humans thought wondrous but were really quite common in the horse world? You told me you wished I could speak. Well, I can, to those who listen.

"If you had told me three years ago in Edinburgh what I would be doing now, I would have thought: 'Crumbs, I am like a fairy tale character come alive!' "

The sunlight shimmered through the heavy green leaves of Hyde Park and across the mammoth roundabout where hundreds of cars were weaving themselves paths to reach six turnings. Beyond lay the 40-acre walled garden of the great quadrangle of Buckingham Palace.

The rays shone on the big horse brilliantly painted in brown, white and black. His coat gleamed like rich velvet.

"I will tell you my story"

Cicero nudged my pocket.

"Another sugar lump is in order," he said. "You should feel no hesitation in giving it to me although, as you say, a carrot would probably be more healthful. I practised particularly well this morning."

His brown eyes beamed. They were so large and luminous—as well as friendly and sensible—that I hurried to comply. His big pink and grey lips carefully scooped up the gift from my open palm.

"You see, no slobber, no mess," he said. "After all, I am now a gentleman of the Queen's Life Guards and I must watch my deportment. Mind you, they tell me I seem to have a natural pride in doing things well.

"Make yourself at home and I will tell you my story. You will see how the most extraordinary events can happen, and, whenever a little special care is taken, life really can be transformed into something very wonderful."

(left) Cicero . . . was extremely curious and eager to see all he could

(below) "Sometimes I do miss Ireland's rich green grass"

2 *My Early Days*

"I was born eight years ago near Armagh in Northern Ireland," said Cicero, his voice taking on a different, somewhat dreamy tone.

Ahah! I thought. So many marvellous horses come from Ireland.

"I really don't remember much about my early days," he went on, "although sometimes I do miss Ireland's rich green grass. I have heard people say it looks good enough to eat. Well, I can tell you, it is!

"I've had nothing like that for a long while. Even the hot mashes the troopers fix up for us every afternoon here at the barracks in winter don't come up to that. But I am digressing . . ."

Cicero told how he used to be hitched to a plough to turn the soil on a small farm not far from Armagh, where both the Catholic and Protestant archbishops of all Ireland live. It was sod over which Patrick, Ireland's patron saint, had walked . . . Time moves slowly in Ireland and Cicero's work was not too hard.

"I liked the children best," he said. "My bright colouring—I am a skewbald, you know—singled me out for some special notice, and, although life was not easy, I had a little more attention than some of my mates."

The days went on, one much like another. Then one day he was brought in from the field, and, with just a rope halter, was walked up and down before a dealer from town.

"Ah, yes," the man said, "young, a good size, a docile disposition, I'll have him."

Pounds changed hands. In a few moments the big horse was being sped by van to the nearest docks.

"I might tell you my heart was in my mouth," said Cicero. "That's what people say, isn't it, when they mean they feel fear?

"But I soon stuffed that feeling down. I flinched when cars passed, though. I wasn't accustomed to them.

"The van was open and I could look out at the green fields. I began feeling a little exhilaration because of the movement—so fleet and yet from no effort of my own. I remember the wind blowing round my face. I enjoyed that. I hadn't given myself a good rubbing against a tree for some time. I didn't know what it was to be groomed then. I braced myself—just as I do now when I am standing still on the parade ground and my drummer-rider is banging away at my kettle drums and we're doing the royal salute."

The van stopped beside an open corral near docks where the sea rolled, all grey-green and foaming.

Quite a few horses were there already—a motley lot; mostly bays and chestnuts of mixed breeding. Bruised shoulders revealed years of drawing ploughs and carts.

It was early September and, thanks to Ireland's succulent green grass, most of them were looking their humble best. Some had been summer-fattened for the slaughterhouses of those great eaters of horsemeat, the Belgians and the French, but were fortunately unaware of their destination.

For most, the strangeness of their present situation was just part of the daily grind to which they had become inured. But Cicero, only four years old and so little experienced in the ways of the world, was extremely curious and eager to see all he could. As he was the only spotted horse a few persons pointed him out. But for most of the passers-by, he—with his rough coat, big dirty hairy hooves, wispy mane and tail—was just one of a forlorn little group prodded into the hold of a ship bound for Scotland.

"I don't know if you ever have crossed the Irish Sea," Cicero remarked. "But I'm sure if you have, you would rather be up on top in the fresh air than in the depths of the ship. I cannot tell you the misery of being down in the hold. The sea was terribly rough. My companions had difficulty in keeping on their feet. One was badly cut on the shoulder. I took a wide stance, balancing as best I could. One of the sailors exclaimed: 'Look at that spotted one! He's got sea legs.'"

It seemed like days but it was only hours until the horses were pulled, pushed and heaved ashore.

"I moved off on my own legs, thank you," said Cicero. "We hadn't much time on land, however, until four of us were sorted out and sent off by van."

A van, this time a closed one, took Cicero across Scotland to Edinburgh—a short trip but one of the noisiest experiences Cicero had yet had.

"On that ride," he said, "I had my first encounter with heavy traffic, something I am supposed to handle without a qualm now. The noise, the exhaust smell, the whoosh of passing vehicles, the sense of terrible, unfeeling, relentless force was awful. Those were my lowest moments."

The journey ended at a field on the outskirts of Edinburgh. The shaky-kneed horse, tired and thoroughly dispirited, clambered out on to the grass.

"I must say it was good to feel solid earth," Cicero said. "The grass looked like heaven, although it had been heavily grazed and wasn't much to chew on—not like the tender, juicy, tasty grass I had been used to. Nevertheless, I was resolved to make the most of things."

*It was a windy cold day for September . . . Mr. Stoddart (left) who knew Mr. Stevenson well . . .
proposed a fair price of £120*

3 St. Cuthbert's

Cicero and his friends were in a field belonging to A. K. Stoddart, a longtime Edinburgh cattle dealer. His meat office is at the city's large slaughterhouse, but he also imports working and riding horses and, as a hobby, has at his home a fine collection of saddlery and harness.

The horses didn't graze long before Mr. Stoddart appeared with a prospective buyer.

"I wasn't at my best," Cicero recalled. "I was snivelling with a cold. Usually I am happy to see people but I am afraid I largely ignored what went on."

The prospective buyer was William Stevenson, transport head of St. Cuthbert's Co-operative Association, which still finds it more profitable to use horses than motors for milk deliveries in the quarter of Edinburgh near its century-old main office because there is no city tax on horse-drawn vehicles.

Mr. Stevenson, sturdy, kind, shrewd and cautious, had worked it out to the last penny. As long as he could get good stable hands and drivers, the dairy was best served by horses in this particular part of the town. Thus, from time to time, Mr. Stevenson called upon Mr. Stoddart to obtain a suitable carthorse for him.

It was a windy, cold day for September, a fine rain was falling and Mr. Stevenson wasn't long in making his choice. Cicero took his eye at once. Also a big bay, Mr. Stevenson looked at their teeth and asked how much the two horses would cost. Mr. Stoddart, who knew Mr. Stevenson well, and neither liked haggling, proposed a fair price of £120 each.

"One hundred twenty each," Mr. Stevenson repeated. "I'll take them!"

Cicero rather liked the sound of his mellow Scots voice.

A horse box appeared. Cicero and the big bay climbed in. Soon they were rumbling towards the city. More traffic noises again. The vehicle lurched now and again. Cicero, used to it by now, braced himself.

Up a rise they went, full of smoky old buildings near the steeply stepped plateau formed by the dark old castle rock. The van turned into St. Cuthbert's main courtyard—a wide open space edged by warehouses and scores of motorised delivery vans painted red and inscribed "St. Cuthbert's" in large letters.

The horses were unloaded and walked along a cobblestone street and then down a busy main road to turn again, and once again, into a kind of warehouse with a ramp leading to an upper floor, where some twenty-five horses occupied individual stalls.

"By this time," Cicero said, "I was really worn out. Mr. Stevenson appeared. I was glad to see him. A man with him went over me and gave me something for the cold."

Mr. Stevenson stood looking at him.

"He's a big fellow," Mr. Stevenson said. "I think we should put him in a loosebox, not a stall."

That meant Cicero would have quarters big enough to move freely in and he would not have to wear a halter. There seemed to be only one other loosebox, which was next door and occupied by a giant black intent upon watching everything that was going on.

"I had a good bed of straw and plenty of company nearby—lots of snorting and stamping—and some good hay in the manger," Cicero went on. "A stableman gave me a rubdown which felt great and then poured some interesting stuff, oats and bran probably, into my feed box. Life was looking better."

The next morning Cicero felt more like himself. Some of his old sense of well being had returned.

"He's been broken in but has never worked in town," Mr. Stevenson told Stable Foreman Jimmie Macdonald. "I think you had better harness him to an empty milk lorry and walk at his head around the streets for a time."

Cicero hated it at first. He had to wear more harness than anything he had known in Ireland. The eye blinkers limited his sight. He never knew what was going past him until it was well ahead. And the noise! Would he ever become accustomed to that?

But he made no trouble. A rubdown on his return helped raise his spirits. One day before long, he pulled away with a rubber-tyred, four-wheeled milk float—St. Cuthbert's refer only to two wheelers as "carts"—and forty cases of milk bottles weighing a ton.

Running beside him was his new driver—an agile, alert man, wearing a jaunty blue wool stocking cap with a tassel on the top. Wullie Wilson, forty-six years with St. Cuthbert's, was both experienced and kind. He seldom used his horse's reins while on deliveries. His voice and the brake were enough.

"Get along, Paddy," Wullie said.

The blinkers limited Cicero's sight

Cicero, still blinkered, enjoys some good hay

An agile alert man wearing a jaunty blue wool stocking cap with a tassel on the top—Wullie Wilson, forty-six years with St. Cuthbert's

"When Wullie loosed it, I'd start again"

4 *Wullie*

At St. Cuthbert's, every new horse from Ireland is called Paddy. Wullie Wilson had known many Paddies.

"Wullie is quite a man," Cicero said, his Scots brogue more noticeable than ever. "At first Wullie let me know what was wanted by just a word or two but he would run beside the small brake wheel, and, before long, when he turned it, I would hear it and stop, and when he loosed it, I'd start again. Never a wasted word, or act, with Wullie. Unlike some drivers, he never thoughtlessly parked me and my heavy load on a hill without the brake well on."

These first months were varied only by the weather. Cicero, because of Wullie's alert ways, quickly became accustomed to the traffic along his eight-mile route, even in Gorgie Road, a main thoroughfare in this grimy industrial end of the town.

The winter days were often wet and slippery and so dark that the day's work, which began at 4 or 5, was half finished before it became light.

"I didn't mind," Cicero said. "Wullie usually had something amusing to say. The way he kept darting up and down stairs, pulling the full bottles out of cases and dropping the empties in and taking me by my blinkered bridle across busy streets impressed me with the importance of our operation.

"There was even something wonderful about the snowy days when the white flakes veiled the old grey tenement houses and a bitterly cold wind would blow the snow straight into my face. Snow never bothered Wullie, either. He said he had been in the navy during the war. After that, the elements never daunted him."

"Only one thing kept bothering me," Cicero went on. "That was paper blowing about the streets. Perhaps the blinkers made it worse. Bits would suddenly fly up round my nose, whizzing here and there and I would rear straight up and the milk bottles would go crash! Wullie would come rushing up. 'De'il tak' it! ! !' he would say."

15

Cicero soon knew every stop. Some customers would run down the flights of stone steps common to the tall tenement houses with a last minute order and would break into smiles when they saw the big, gentle, spotted horse standing there.

Some saved potato peelings for him. Others brought carrots. The corner grocer came out with bruised vegetables. Elderly men out for their morning walk and elderly women on their way for a loaf of bread used to stop for a friendly pat. On Saturdays the children gathered.

The treats enlivened the morning, but Wullie was particular about what Cicero was offered. He said "no" to crusts of bread. "Not good for horses," he would explain.

One warm day in the spring, a little girl handed Cicero the end of her ice cream cone—his first confrontation with ice cream. He decided it was good, very good!

"Incidentally, come to think of it, ice cream is another thing I miss in London," Cicero said.

"I think I really got Wullie into trouble only once," Cicero continued. "One day I spied a lady coming towards me holding an enormous ice cream cone, as the Scots call it.

"As she passed, I reached forward—like this—and deftly licked the ice cream off the cone—so.

"She didn't realise what was happening until she saw the empty cone. She screamed. How she screamed! I was so embarrassed. The ice cream had already slipped delightfully down my throat. There wasn't very much I could do about it!"

Wullie apologised to the lady, who having been properly introduced to "Paddy", and once over the initial shock, was pleased he had enjoyed her treat!

But for Wullie an apology was not enough.

"Chocolate or vanilla?" Wullie insisted. Then into the nearest café he ran to buy her another cone.

"I think the ice cream episode taught me a lesson," Cicero said. "It's much more pleasant to be offered something. You don't happen to have something more about yourself to offer me just now? No? Perhaps it's just as well."

(right) "One day," said Cicero
demonstrating, "I spied a lady . . ."

(below) "I reached forward like this . . ."

"and deftly lifted the ice cream . . ."

"How she screamed! I was so embarrassed!"

Mr. Stevenson was discussing the finer points of a carriage . . .

5 *The Meeting*

Watered and rubbed down every afternoon when he came in from his milk round, Cicero was beginning to have a greater sense of well being. He came to love St. Cuthbert's.

Occasionally when he and Wullie rattled into St. Cuthbert's courtyard they would see several of the other milk horses hitched to strange looking coaches, some hooded and enclosed, some with open seats and steps.

Generals, ladies, brides and sometimes mourners use St. Cuthbert's more lithe looking greys, blacks and bays, so stable in traffic, for ceremonial events.

"I thought a coach like one of those would be rather grand," Cicero said. "But Wullie, as though guessing what was going through my mind, tartly commented that that sort of thing was not for a heavy legged, half-plough, spotted horse like me!"

One afternoon in June, Wullie and Cicero clattered with the empties into the courtyard, their day's work done. A Stranger with a moustache, his tweed suit impeccably pressed, was discussing with Mr. Stevenson the finer points of a carriage fresh from St. Cuthbert's own wagon works and resplendent in maroon.

"Ah, a skewbald," said the Stranger, his attention diverted by Cicero's arrival. "Let me have a good look at him."

"Height is right, 17 hands," the Stranger mused. "Colour, too."

Wullie and Cicero continued into the shed to deposit the milk float. When they came out, with Cicero still in his harness and Wullie's hand on his bridle ready for the scamper through the traffic and around to the stable, the two men still were talking.

A few days passed. Cicero's afternoon rubdown seemed to be getting longer and longer. One day he didn't go out on his round at all. Instead he had the grooming of his life.

"You're going to the Palace of Holyroodhouse to see the Queen," said Stable Chief

Stableman John Kemp chose the best rope halter St. Cuthbert's had

Down the hill from the ancient Castle edged by grey-black six- and seven-storey buildings

(right) *A unicorn in stone watched haughtily*

(left) *Off into the stable yard*

Macdonald, once a trooper with the Scots Greys, who had since exchanged their beautiful Greys for clanking tanks and armoured cars. "You must look your best."

There was a stir of excitement in the stables. Even the big black, Centenary, the senior and most privileged horse, was impressed. He, coming long ago from Friesland, was St. Cuthbert's greatest star. He seemed about 20 hands tall and loomed over his loosebox, three times the size of the stalls.

A rope halter was put round Cicero's head—Stableman John Kemp chose the best one St. Cuthbert's had. Mr. Stevenson himself took charge and quietly urged Cicero up into a horse van.

"Another trip, I thought," Cicero said.

It was a short journey—only down the hill from the ancient Castle edged by grey-black, six and seven-storey buildings—some of the earliest skyscrapers in Europe—along the cobblestones of the "Royal Mile" to black wrought-iron gates and into the broad courtyard of Holyroodhouse, a grey stone palace set amid green grass lawns at the foot of the seven hills surrounding Edinburgh.

Instead of drawing up at the main entrance, where a unicorn in stone watched haughtily from atop a pillar, the van turned off into the stable yard. Here a little group of men, including the Stranger, awaited. Mr. Stevenson led Cicero out of the van.

The Stranger doffed his hat—but not to Cicero. The Queen had walked in through the mews gate.

"She had a scarf on her head," Cicero said. "Not a crown."

"Here is the horse, Ma'am," the Stranger said.

The Queen walked around Cicero, looking carefully, saying nothing, half smiling.

She scrutinised his countenance, looking him in the eyes. Then she rubbed his nose. Cicero could see her eyes warm to a bright blue.

"I knew she liked me," Cicero said.

The Queen talked for a minute with the Stranger, who was Colonel John Miller, a member of the Royal Household known as the crown equerry and responsible for all the Queen's horses. She smiled goodbye and walked into the palace.

Half an hour later, Cicero was back at St. Cuthbert's.

The next morning when Wullie came for him to go out on his round as usual, Cicero was Paddy no longer.

"Come on, Drummer," Wullie said.

"Drum horses don't grow on bushes," Wullie observed

6 *The Major*

It was settled—or so it seemed. St. Cuthbert's big spotted milk horse with the genial manner had been looked upon with favour by the Queen. Word spread that the Queen was buying him to become a royal drum horse in London.

Candidates for this special role in the great state occasions were difficult to find. They had to be a "paint" or colour horse. They had to be 17 hands.

"Drum horses don't grow on bushes," Wullie observed.

As a drum horse, Cicero would become the chief ornament of the Queen's Household Cavalry, which glories in having served as the sovereign's bodyguard ever since Charles II returned from exile in Holland to recover the throne that Cromwell had taken from his father.

At St. Cuthbert's, it was "Drummer" this and "Drummer" that. Cicero went about his daily milk deliveries with extra pride now that all this extra interest was being taken in him.

The men were pleased and proud their milk horse had won the approval of the sovereign. But was it not appropriate?

St. Cuthbert's had begun to be useful to the Royal Household after the Queen's coronation when she paid her state visit to Edinburgh. It was then that the Scottish crown jewels, "the Honours of Scotland", were taken out of Edinburgh Castle and paraded by carriage through the city.

The palace at that time was in desperate need of carriage horses used to traffic and of men to drive them to carry the jewels and officers of state like the Lord Lyon, Scotland's white-maned chief herald, superb in his golden tabard.

To the aid of the Queen on this supreme occasion came the milk men and the milk horses of St. Cuthbert's, all so expert in traffic, all so accustomed to crowds, all so unflappable in emergency, transporting with great style Scotland's own centuries-old crown, sword and sceptre through the streets lined with crowds.

27

All had gone without mishap. The venerable Jock and Silver, both greys, had walked, Cicero heard, like chargers of old amid the handclaps, the skirl of the pipes and the crash of the drums.

Since that day, a bond between the Royal Household and St. Cuthbert's had flourished. Royal carriages were transported for maintenance at St. Cuthbert's, now appointed coach painters to the Queen!

"But this glow of pleasure didn't last," Cicero said.

One day when Cicero and Wullie drove into St. Cuthbert's, their day's work done, a New Stranger was pacing up and down. He was a major from The Blues (now The Blues and Royals), one of the two Household Cavalry regiments, the other being The Life Guards. He had come to inspect Cicero.

The Major studied Cicero. He scowled. He was not impressed.

"Won't do, won't do at all," snapped the Major. "I'm turning him down on conformation. Horrid."

There were other words too; Cicero had a "ridge back", a "goose rump".

It all sounded so undignified that I winced and urged Cicero to get on with the story.

"Well," said Cicero, "the Major, whose name we won't mention, strode off. Wullie had an angry glint in his eyes. Mr. Stevenson could have said: 'The Queen, who knows horses, likes him'. But he didn't. My hind quarters did slant. Perhaps I had been pulling loads too long."

Wullie led Cicero into the milk lorry shed.

"Come on, Paddy," Wullie said.

By appointment coachpainters to the Queen

7 *On Trial*

Could a major's opinion count more than that of a queen, especially this queen, so knowledgeable about horses?

"I weighed the question," Cicero said.

Ten months passed. Cicero daily drew his milk lorry. Glasgow's mounted police acquired the big bay, Cicero's companion from Ireland. Mr. Stevenson, though sorry to see a good milk horse go, was pleased St. Cuthbert's could help Glasgow. Did not St. Cuthbert's Co-operative Association firmly believe:

"The control of humans can still be most effectively performed by the employment of our noble friend, the horse . . ."

Then it was June and the Queen was again at Holyroodhouse. Colonel Miller reappeared at St. Cuthbert's.

"Have you still got the big skewbald?" the Colonel asked Mr. Stevenson.

Events moved quickly. This time there was no preliminary inspection by the Household Cavalry. Colonel F. H. Orr, Commandant of the Royal Army Veterinary Corps Training Centre at Melton Mowbray, came to St. Cuthbert's, examined Cicero inch by inch and, taking him by the halter, ran back and forth with him, testing wind and movement. Medically he saw no problem.

But Cicero could see the Colonel had doubts. Every time his skilled eyes passed over Cicero's rear, they clouded, but they brightened when they fell on Cicero's fine head and shoulders.

"Perhaps training will improve him," Colonel Orr said.

The Colonel told Mr. Stevenson his price, £120, was very reasonable.

"We don't want to make money on a transaction with our Queen," said Mr. Stevenson, who had bought Cicero from Mr. Stoddart for the same amount. "We have had a year's labour from the horse."

Cicero was "Drummer" again!

"When he stops pulling, he will stop dipping," the men of St. Cuthbert's said.

A few days later Cicero stepped out of a horse box at Colonel Orr's 300-acre Royal

Colonel Orr of the Royal Army Veterinary Corps Training Centre at Melton Mowbray

Army Veterinary Corps Training Centre amid the green fields surrounding Melton Mowbray.

"A marvellous place," Cicero said. "More grass than I'd seen for a long time."

For two weeks Cicero was quarantined at the hospital and plied with vitamins and other things for strengthening and purifying him.

"I felt as though I was being turned inside out," Cicero said. "And do you know what they called me? 5935! I had become a number. That's the Army for you!"

Cicero was turned out to pasture with a half dozen blacks also destined for the Household Cavalry. Cicero tweaked their tails and pulled their hair.

"I don't know what got into me," he said. "Perhaps it was all that grass."

So the Colonel put Cicero into a small field by himself. A young groom, Private Angela Tucker, began dropping around for a daily chat.

"That angel Angela," said Cicero. "How she admired me!"

"Would you like to ride him?" asked the Colonel. "Be sure you walk him up and down hills to strengthen his hind quarters."

It was an interesting time. One of his neighbours, a bay, dislocated her neck jumping.

"The end," people said.

But the Colonel put her in a sling and in time she was kicking her heels again.

There also was Sabrina, the beautiful grey. She had gone to London to carry a trumpeter but she couldn't get used to all that tooting. She had failed. But the Colonel welcomed her back and developed her into a fine show jumper.

"I heard," Cicero said, "that during the war the Colonel was responsible for 22,000 horses and mules on the Burma Road. You can't get more experience than that."

After five months, the Colonel pronounced 5935 ready for London. Cicero was given his first formal bath.

"Shampoo and all," said Cicero. "Even a drier. It was a big room with heaters pouring out hot air from overhead. It was lovely!"

There was just one thing more—new shoes. The Colonel had discovered Cicero was a quarter of an inch short of the required 17 hands. Only 16 hands three inches and three quarters!

"But he had a remedy," Cicero said. "The blacksmith made special shoes an extra quarter of an inch thick!"

On a cold January day, Cicero arrived in London to join The Life Guards. He saw eyebrows rise and heard one trooper ask Riding Master Captain Alec Jackson if he thought the new recruit would "make it".

"Well, we'll try," the Captain replied.

"My look had become important . . . I had to develop an air, a presence, a consciousness of grandeur"

8 *The Recruit*

"I must say I was impressed," Cicero said.

His new London home was a row of cream buildings with Grecian pillars and pediments called Wellington Barracks just round the corner from Buckingham Palace.

On closer inspection the barracks looked rather uncomfortable. His stable was a makeshift structure built to serve until the new Knightsbridge cavalry barracks was completed on its old site in Hyde Park.

But he had a big loosebox to himself labelled with his new name, CICERO, printed in large letters. Drum horses are always given grand names, preferably ancient ones, he discovered.

"I liked that," Cicero said.

He was assigned his own groom, Trooper John Barrass, 22, from Yorkshire, and his own trainer, Corporal Barry McKie, 24, from Somerset.

"I was fortunate again with the people I fell in with," Cicero said. "How that new young man groomed me, washing me down almost daily. He worked on my coat and mane and tail and hooves. Instead of trimming my hair short around my hooves as they did at St. Cuthbert's to keep it out of the splash from the streets, he cultivated my 'feathers', billowed my tail, encouraged my skimpy mane. You see, my look had become important. I had to develop what they call an air, a presence, a consciousness of grandeur."

His trainer led Cicero into the temporary riding school. Tall, thin, a devotee of horses from the age of nine when he began riding under the eyes of an ex-Life Guards trooper, the Corporal treated Cicero, equipped only with a halter, as if he never had been handled before.

"I had to forget all I had been taught and begin at the beginning as if I were a baby," said Cicero. "In fact," and his voice constricted slightly, "that is how the officers

"John billowed my tail"

The Corporal added a saddle

John had a kind, careful way

sometimes addressed me—me, a full grown six-year-old, with more than a year's experience in public service!"

The Corporal set Cicero moving in a circle, first this way and then that, on the lunge rein, to strengthen the muscles around the spine and to gain Cicero's trust and respect.

"I liked his voice," Cicero said. "It was slow and quiet. Like Wullie, the Corporal used only a few words."

"Walk on" meant a nice, bold pace. "Whoa" meant stop at once. In a while the command "trot" was added. Then "canter". Soon, Cicero was moving, like a car, from gear to gear, from walk to trot to canter and back again.

Occasionally, when Cicero baulked, the Corporal said reproachfully: "Now, Cis!"

"I used to get 'a bit Bolshie', as the Corporal would say, and buck and play around before settling down to work," Cicero said. "I like a little fun and I pretended to run away. The Corporal would understand that. He wanted me to have a little relaxation. But I grew to understand that there was a time for work and a time for play."

In a few weeks, Corporal McKie added a training strap around Cicero's middle to accustom him to a girth and by the end of the third month, a saddle.

"He said he didn't want to frighten me—as if he could," Cicero said. "So he had himself lifted into the saddle."

Cicero took this development literally in his stride.

"By that time I had seen so many men on horses' backs," Cicero said, "I had begun to wonder why I was being left out!

"But I had become so used to pulling a load and wearing blinkers that it took some time before I could round corners without making a wide allowance for the milk float."

He learned, at a tap behind the shoulder, to "stand out", the "at attention" stance, with forelegs set well forward side by side. The Corporal looked at mirrors set high on the walls to check how well Cicero was doing it.

One April morning they ventured into the street. They moved at a good pace down Birdcage Walk, named after the aviary Charles II kept in St. James's Park.

"I didn't mind the traffic," Cicero said. "No worse than Edinburgh, although, without blinkers, I took some time getting used to seeing so much going on. Sometimes people slowed their cars to greet us."

All summer the Corporal alternated days between work in the riding school and walking out in the streets. Sometimes, for a change, Cicero had an early morning trot around Rotten Row amid the leafy greenery of Hyde Park, with either the Corporal in the saddle or lean, neat John.

"I liked that!" Cicero said.

With John on an early morning tramp through Hyde Park

In October, John, in his kind, careful way, buckled two aluminium kettle drums, painted a dull brown, on Cicero's shoulders and fastened a pair of reins to the Corporal's boots, so he could guide Cicero with his feet while beating the drums.

"Noisy but rather different," Cicero said.

One day, right in the middle of Parliament Square below Big Ben, the Corporal said: "Whoa, Cis! Stand out!"

"We stayed there for a long time," Cicero said, "with traffic passing on all sides. I was very interested in all that went on. It didn't bother me at all. When I returned to the barracks, I had a feeling I had done especially well."

Cicero with the practice drums sets off to brave the traffic

"I had a feeling I had done especially well," said Cicero on returning to the barracks

9 *Disaster*

Cicero was feeling rather smart when The Life Guards and The Blues and Royals moved to the new barracks in Hyde Park late in October.

"A four million pound structure," Cicero said. "Nothing like it in all the world. Air conditioned, running water, heated ramps so we won't slide on the winter ice, troopers sleeping near to tend us, a whole skyscraper for families. What do you think of that?"

He was not pleased, however, with his own quarters.

"John put me in a stall—me!" Cicero said. "I was flabbergasted. How could he have done that to me! I dealt with that situation immediately."

Cicero tossed his head, broke the halter, backed out, trotted down the line of stalls and was almost in the Stable yard before someone caught him.

John came with a new halter and put him back in the same stall.

"Why, Cis!" he said.

Cicero promptly broke the second halter and again made his way out. This time John again put on a new halter but he led Cicero to a big loosebox at the far end of the stalls. It was marked "CICERO" in capital letters but, as the door fastening was broken, John earlier had decided to have it repaired before Cicero took possession of his new home.

"You're getting too full of yourself, Cis!" John said.

"Why accept a room when you're accustomed to a suite?" Cicero asked me.

Cicero learned about a new part of the city. Sometimes he and the Corporal joined the heavy traffic in fashionable Knightsbridge or added a live statue to swirling Hyde Park Corner. In the grand new riding school, where the Corporal could open and close the doors from the saddle with only the press of a button, he banged the aluminium drums more loudly each week.

Cicero heard about his famous predecessors—Pompey, greatly mourned, who had died

"Whew! For a moment I thought my legs would buckle"

John had to shorten Cicero's "at attention" stance

shortly after the Queen's coronation, and Alexander the Great, sorely lamented and also recently departed.

"Alex's mane was so long it reached his knees and, when he bent his head, it touched the ground," Cicero said. "But he slipped coming down the cobblestones from Edinburgh Castle. He hadn't my experience on those streets. They say here that I have a particularly solid and sure pace. Experience does tell, you know."

Very Important Persons from different parts of the world visited the barracks. One such day Cicero was put on show. John, with the Corporal already in the saddle, strapped on the great ceremonial drums of solid silver, a gift from King William IV almost a century and a half ago.

Each drum weighs 56 pounds.

"Whew! For a moment I thought my legs would buckle," Cicero said.

"Walk on, Cis," the Corporal said.

But Cicero was stuck. He had to bring up his hind legs before he could move forward.

So for the next weeks he had to learn to shorten his "at attention" stance to balance the drums.

In March, disaster struck.

"Right in the middle of the Stable yard," Cicero said, "where everybody could see me—from our Major, John Fuller, downwards."

A Stranger mounted Cicero. The practice aluminium drums were strapped on. But, instead of the Corporal's discordant bangs, the Stranger crashed into the sonorous, rhythmical notes of the royal fanfare.

"I jumped straight up," Cicero said. "The man stayed on but he stopped playing."

He was Life Guards drummer Bernie Moore who, dressed in his gold coat and blue velvet jockey cap, was to ride Cicero and play the silver drums in June at the Trooping the Colour ceremony on the Queen's official birthday, high point of the Household Cavalry's year.

The Corporal, aghast, decreed an hour workout.

"You can't get away with that," the Corporal said, sternly.

"I might say the whole affair was highly disagreeable," Cicero said. "I let them know I didn't like it, too."

John, who once confided he never liked horses until he knew Cicero, sadly took him into the stable, saying:

"If you don't get used to the drummer, you won't make the grade—and what can they do with you at Melton Mowbray!"

Cicero under the strain of the two silver drums each weighing 56 pounds

Welcome relief! John is about to remove the drums

10 *The Silver Drums*

Cicero's career was at a crossroads. He would put back his ears, even when the Corporal was riding him and bashing the drums in his usual way.

He banged his stable door and tried to boss John and the Corporal in a way which touched on the unmannerly.

"The Corporal said I had to develop an ear for music," Cicero went on. " 'Get rhythm', he said. Or there would be no silver drums for me, no drum horse career, no Trooping the Colour before the Queen."

One day Cicero gave his stable door such a bang that it came right off.

"They didn't like that, at all," Cicero said.

John moved Cicero to a loosebox nearby which had a single thick iron bar instead of a door.

"There, try that," said John, his pleasant voice touched with firmness.

For the drummer, this Trooping was to be especially memorable because it was to be his last before leaving the army. The Corporal and John were beginning to worry that the Trooping might not be Cicero's first.

Twice weekly, the drummer and Nicholas Slater, his understudy, attempted to practise playing the aluminium drums on Cicero, but with little success. The Corporal wouldn't trust Cicero with the silver drums, which might get bashed on the wrong places.

Day after day the Corporal rode Cicero and banged away at the aluminium drums and, sometimes, even at the silver ones. Cicero tolerated him. But when either of the drummers was in the saddle, Cicero pawed the air.

Trooper Barrass and Corporal McKie were full of concern. They daily consulted together, trying to discover what disturbed Cicero the moment the drummer began drumming.

"I could have told them if they'd only have listened," Cicero said. "It was a White

Cicero, with his drummer in State dress, marches past the Queen

Something—like paper—that whizzed about overhead every time the drummer began to play. The Corporal and John kept watching and, in time, figured it out for themselves."

"The white ends of the drumsticks!" they exclaimed, almost like one.

"It's the way Moore flashes them high, holds them there for a moment and then crashes down!"

The Corporal leaped into the saddle and swooped the sticks high as Moore did, instead of keeping them low. Cicero danced an angry jig.

"But the Corporal and John showed me what this whiteness was and kept flashing it around me," Cicero said. "For weeks they bothered me, whisking those white things everywhere. After a while I grew to consider them part of the exercise, although it was a long time before I ceased thinking about them."

In April, Cicero's testing time came with the massed bands of The Life Guards and The Blues and Royals. With the drummer in the saddle, John strapped on the silver drums.

For the first time, Cicero stood out grandly in their midst, the great drums glittering on his shoulders.

It was only a rehearsal for the massed bands, one of the many before the Trooping in June. But for Cicero it was his passing-out test. If he conducted himself well, he would be a recruit no longer but a graduate Drum Horse of The Life Guards.

The drummer-musician raised the sticks high and whammed into the royal salute. The notes rang rich and deep and true.

"How noble the sound was," Cicero said. "I don't know if it was the tone of the silver drums or the challenging presence of The Blues and Royals (We, in The Life Guards, call them The Other Regiment), but I didn't stir. A feeling of great enjoyment came over me. Everything was going to be all right."

At two performances of a lesser ceremony called Beating Retreat, Cicero became familiar with the big parade ground called "Horseguards", between Whitehall and St. James's Park, where the Trooping was to take place.

At the first performance there, a slight tumult arose as the white-plumed head-dresses of The Life Guards, instead of bobbing ceremoniously up and down, for a minute became like a surge of ocean spray.

"I am glad to say that it was one of the trumpeters' greys, not I, who was shaking off his rider," said Cicero.

At the second Retreat Cicero, with his white feathers flying, proudly for the first time paced with his silver drums past the Queen, who was there on a platform to take the salute.

"I'm glad I didn't have blinkers on," said Cicero. "I could see it all."

5—C * *

A close-up of some members of Cicero's regiment in their ceremonial dress, this time in Windsor

Cicero was quite composed the morning of the Trooping, held yearly in June even though the Queen's real birthday is in April, on this same large open space behind the arches in Whitehall, where two mounted troopers guard the headquarters of the Household Division on the site of the old Palace of Whitehall, burned down in 1698 in the reign of William III.

"It was John, who had a shock that morning," said Cicero. "It happened while John was accoutering me in my ceremonial garb, consisting of the heavy, padded saddle; the breastplate with the Star of the Garter, the Queen's most exclusive order of knighthood; the body cloth embroidered in gold with the regimental battle honours; the elaborate head kit with its insignias of a major; two bits; two sets of gold threaded reins; the silver drums, their many straps, their richly decorated draperies.

"At the last moment a brush ornament hanging like a pendant from my neck went to bits—it simply broke up in John's hand."

John rushed to the storeroom for a replacement. It was difficult to find. The suspense was awful. But not for Cicero.

"After all, who notices that piece of my array," said Cicero. "But, for John, it was an essential part of my uniform. He found another and we were at the appropriate mounting block in the Stable yard in good time. There, the drummer, in his gold attire of state, climbed on, John gave us a last adjustment or two and we were ready."

The Life Guards and The Blues and Royals moved out of the barracks, down along Hyde Park and past Buckingham Palace, where they were joined by the Queen, mounted and wearing the scarlet coat of a Colonel of the Grenadier Guards (whose colour was being trooped on that occasion), and a deep blue riding skirt and small black three-cornered hat. She, too, wore the Garter Star.

Thousands edged the broad Mall between the palace and the parade ground, where a thousand scarlet-clad footguards were lined up, waiting.

More thousands of onlookers filled stands built along the three sides of Horseguards.

The Household Cavalry—including the big horse advancing so solidly and proudly as he made his début—took their place along the fourth open side of the huge rectangle, against the magic greenery of St. James's Park.

The Brigade clock in its tower merrily chimed 11 o'clock as the Queen rode on to the parade ground.

Cicero's most difficult part was to stay still for almost an hour.

"I did grow restless standing off to one side like that—doing nothing while those footguards marched and countermarched," he said.

At last the horseguards' turn came. The troopers clattered past first in a walk and then

The Queen enters the parade ground for the Trooping

in a trot. Cicero's drummer vied with the cannon in Hyde Park in the explosive enthusiasm of the birthday salute.

"It was all rather gorgeous," Cicero said.

He had not counted on all that extra booming of royal salutes from cannons in the Park and at the Tower nor, later, on those jet planes flying low in salute overhead, nor on those masses of people who had come to see the Queen on horseback, but everything had gone off well.

★   ★   ★

I stirred. It was time to go.

"Wouldn't you agree no one ever gave you a more exclusive interview?" asked Cicero. "By the way, how about a sugar lump now?"

I just happened to have one. Delicately he lifted it from my hand. He chomped it for a while, making it last, and then, pausing, said reflectively:

"I'm so glad they named me Cicero. I hear he was a great man and he, too, was quite a talker."

"It was all rather gorgeous," Cicero said

PASSING THROVGH THE